GOD,
HELP ME PRAY!

GOD, HELP ME PRAY!

EMAILS TO GOD ON THE TEACHING OF PRAYER FOR TEACHERS AND NEW CHRISTIANS

JERRY L. PARKS,

AUTHOR OF WITH JOSEPH
IN THE UNIVERSITY OF ADVERSITY: THE
MIZRAIM PRINCIPLES, AND DRAGONS,
GRASSHOPPERS & FROGS!

Weekly Reader Press
New York Lincoln Shanghai

GOD, HELP ME PRAY!
EMAILS TO GOD ON THE TEACHING OF PRAYER FOR TEACHERS
AND NEW CHRISTIANS

Copyright © 2006 by Jerry L. Parks

Weekly Reader Press
an imprint of iUniverse, Inc.
and the Weekly Reader Corporation

iUniverse books may be ordered through booksellers or by contacting:

iUniverse
2021 Pine Lake Road, Suite 100
Lincoln, NE 68512
www.iuniverse.com
1-800-Authors (1-800-288-4677)

ISBN-13: 978-0-595-40766-8
ISBN-10: 0-595-40766-8

Printed in the United States of America

CONTENTS

INTRODUCTION

"Prayer is the dove sent out, returned with the olive leaf of peace and joy.
It is the golden chain, which God holds fast, and lets not go till He blesses.
It is the Moses rod, which brings forth the waters of consolation out of the Rock
of Salvation. It is Samson's jawbone, which smites our enemies. It is David's
harp, before which the evil spirits fly. Prayer is the key to Heaven's treasury."

—GERHARDT

Prayer is as simple as talking to God. But sometimes we forget how to listen.

As a young Christian, I never especially looked forward to praying. Too often, I caught myself endlessly repeating formulaic phrases during my evening devotions—and more than once—dozing off on God. But as I got older, I began to understand prayer as far more than a daily ritual. As I studied God's Word, I learned that God keeps our every prayer. I reasoned then, if prayers are so important to God that He *saves* them (Revelation 5:8; 8:4), prayer ought to be important to me also. Eventually praying became a vital communication with the God of Heaven, as well as a necessary channel for that same God to guide me through the perils of living the Christian life in a sinful world. Praying is not always easy. Sometimes it is a labor (Colossians 4:12). But prayer is necessary, and prayer must be done correctly.

This book was written to help you, the Christian, understand how to talk to God, and how to receive His answers. It was not written to answer all the deep theology of prayer, and contains no so-called 'practice' or cookie-cutter formulaic prayers, which do little to express your personal thoughts to God. Rather, the teachings on prayer are merely summarized, and linked to hundreds of Scripture references you would do well to look up and study. This work is not intended to be the final answer on prayer, and the author *is* not, and does not *claim* to be, an expert on this subject. This book is simply the culmination of many years of Bible study, and was inspired by my friend Pat, and the *Adult Bible Fellowship Class* at Southland Christian Church in Lexington, KY.

The book is divided into small sections as follows for easier reading:

❑ *Email message to/from God—*

It is a fearful thing to attempt to speak for God. Nevertheless, what God has *already* spoken can be synthesized into basic theology. Although not meant to be irreverent in any way, these emails attempt to represent how God might answer our questions on prayer, based upon Scripture.

❑ *Principle*

This is the summarized, general teaching from Scripture regarding prayer.

My Blog

My Blog is the personalized, restatement and reminder of the principle.

Homework

➢ 4me2cnsdr.now—these are reflective questions for you to consider.
➢ **To do**—these are calls to action to help you strengthen your prayer life.

Instant message summary

Each chapter concludes with a brief, 'the least you need to know' reminder.

There are many fallacious and shallow works purporting to teach you how you should pray. My hope is that this book will challenge you to develop a new appreciation for the subject of prayer, and begin to pray in a manner most pleasing to God.

To God be the glory.

CHAPTER 1

"WHY PRAY?"
REMEMBERING WHO YOU'RE TALKING TO!

FROM: JERRY
TO: GOD
SUBJECT: WHY PRAY?

God, I'm confused. I understand that you are everywhere, and you know everything. I also know that you love me, and want the best for me, and will do everything you can to give that to me. With all that being true, why should I pray? You already know what I want, you know what I need, and you know what should and will happen, so what's the purpose behind my prayers? I'm sure not going to get you to leave your plan and follow my wishes.

FROM: GOD
TO: JERRY
CC: The Church
SUBJECT: RE: WHY PRAY?

Jerry—I understand your confusion, but I do want you to pray! There's a purpose in prayer. Remember, praying is a part of My plan too. By praying, you are learning some very important lessons. You learn to depend on Me for the answers, you learn to accept My will, and you actually draw nearer to Me through your prayers. This is what I want...you closer to Me. I <u>do</u> love you and want what's best for you!

Principle: Our prayers do have a purpose! Through praying, we are molded more and more into the image of God. Through praying, we learn to live by *His* will, even while expressing to Him our own concerns and our wishes. Through praying, we also open the avenue to thank God for His provision when our prayers are answered.

PRAY TO GLORIFY GOD

The most important reason to pray is to bring glory to your Creator (I Corinthians 10:31). God created you to have fellowship with Him, and so that He could perform His will through your life. A part of His will is that you show Him you recognize how awesome He is (Isaiah 6:1)! God is *holy, just,* and *righteous*. He is the all-powerful One who is both outside and inside time and eternity. He is not Allah, or the universal 'father' of us all (cp. John 8:42-44; cp. Romans 8:9). God is not a glorified Santa Claus waiting for our wish list (Hebrews 10:22). You do not pray to control God as you would a puppet on a string. Neither do you try to force His hand through ritual formula wrapped up in self-will, and call it 'prayer'. Remember Who you're speaking to when you are talking to God (note Isaiah 6:1-7), and appreciate that such a mighty God delights in you coming into His presence (Prov. 15:8).

PRAY BECAUSE GOD TOLD YOU TO

The second most important reason to pray is because God told you to. If for no other reason, you should pray out of obedience to God's instruction (Luke 18:1; I Timothy 2:1; Matthew 6:5), and because such *obedience* reflects your love for the One who saved you. If the God who knows your request even before you ask (Matthew 6:8) still instructs you pray—do it. Remember, pray because God said to.

PRAY BECAUSE YOU LIVE IN A SINFUL WORLD

Someone has said: "You cannot know what prayer is for unless first you know that life is war." We live in a sinful world, and in a human body which has a bent toward sinfulness (Mark 14:38). Because life is a battle between good and evil, darkness and light, and the pull of sin against the desire to please God, you need to keep in touch with the Commander in Chief (Matthew 26:41). Prayer is a part of your battle armor for survival in this sinful world (Ephesians 6:18). Remember, no matter what happens—you're never too *bad*—and it's never too *late*—to pray (cp. Judges 16:28).

PRAY TO EXPRESS YOUR NEEDS TO GOD

This is why most people pray. And God does delight in meeting your needs (Matthew 7:11). But this should be far from the only reason to approach God. When you do come before Him to express the needs and desires of your heart, come in faith and trust that He will answer in the best way possible (Romans 8:28), out of His unlimited resources (Ephesians 1:16; 3:8, 20). Remember, bringing your requests before God should be in an attitude of humility, and show just how much you *need*, *love*, and *appreciate* what only God can do for you.

PRAY TO OPEN A CHANNEL FOR BLESSING

Prayer gives God an opportunity to open a channel of blessing—blessing to *you* through His answering, blessing to *others* because you prayed (I Samuel 12:23), and blessing toward *Him* through your praise and thanksgiving (Psalm 22:3). Answering your prayers even opens a channel for the angels in Heaven to praise God (Ephesians 3:10)! Praise and thanksgiving are not the same, but they are the way you should approach God (Psalm 100:4). As you begin your prayers, *praise* God for who He *is*, but *thank* Him for what He *does*. God would deserve praise even if He never answered one request. Remember that.

PRAY TO AVOID PRIDE AND PRESUMPTION

When you take your concerns to God, you are showing that you depend on Him. The very *act* of prayer evidences humility. Humility is an attitude void of excessive *pride*, (which God hates, Proverbs 6:16-17), and *presumption* (which is sin, Psalm 19:13). God hears prayers offered in humility (Psalm 10:17). He wants you to be *totally* dependent on Him in everything—even your attitude. (See Chapter 10.)

PRAY TO ENJOY FELLOWSHIP WITH GOD

Prayer is a child coming to a loving parent. It is a family privilege that 'outsiders' cannot experience (Proverbs 15:29). God does not need our company. God is perfectly complete in Himself. But still, He enjoys our company through prayer. The famous evangelist Dwight L. Moody once asked his young son why he kept following him around. "Just to be where you are, Daddy" was the reply. Just to adore God and be in His presence should be reason enough to pray. Even if you have nothing to ask God for, pray simply to be in His company.

PRAY TO BE AN INSTRUMENT OF GOD'S PLAN

"Lord, make me an instrument of Your peace" was the prayer of St. Francis of Assisi. You should pray because God can use *you* to bring to pass a part of His eternal plan (Isaiah 6:8). While God does not *need* us to perform His will (Ephesians 1:11), He *uses* us. Can you think of any greater privilege than to be an instrument of God's perfect will? (See Chapter 6.)

PRAY TO SPEED GOD'S WILL!

While we know our prayers *help* bring God's will to pass, did you know there is some evidence that our prayers may even *speed* God's will in coming to pass (Revelation 3:11, 22:20; cp. Isaiah 60:22)? Knowing this, with John, pray for the Lord to come quickly!

My Blog!

Remember, even Jesus prayed! He didn't need to let God know His wishes or thoughts, He certainly didn't need to be forgiven or discover God's will, and yet Jesus spent hours in communion with God. How much *more* should we spend our time communing with the God of the Universe?

Heavenly Homework!

4me2cnsdr.now—

- What personal prayer habits do you have?

- Why do you think God delights in hearing from you even if He's in complete control of all things?

- Which would best describe how you feel about praying: *an obligation, a privilege, a joy,* or *a habit?*

- Which do you think means most to God—praise or thanksgiving? Why?

To do—

- ✓ Make a space in your day to really spend time with God in prayer. Set apart a time that doesn't get filled by daily activities. During this time, pray not only for the everyday things you would pray for, but simply talk to God as if He were a friend, a parent, or a loved one—which He is!

✓ Look up God's 'attributes' (goodness, righteous, holy, etc.) and try praising God for simply Who He *is*.

✓ Think of some things God has done for you, which you may have forgotten to thank Him for. Spend some time doing just that.

✓ Consider right now, how *you* might be the answer to someone else's prayer. Then, go do what you can.

Instant Message Summary:

Praying is talking to the God of the Universe. It is not handing a wish list to Santa Claus. We pray because of need, fellowship, and simply because God told us to. But when you pray, remember Who you're talking to!

CHAPTER 2

"PREPARING YOURSELF TO PRAY"
PLOWING THE WAY BEFOREHAND!

FROM: JERRY
TO: GOD
SUBJECT: HOW DO I GET MYSELF READY TO TALK TO YOU?

God—if we're going to be talking on a regular basis, is there anything I need to do to be sure You and I will be able to communicate? Is there anything I should do to get myself ready to pray? I just hate talking to people who aren't really paying attention, and I want to make sure that doesn't happen with us. What should I do?

TO: JERRY
CC: THE CHURCH
SUBJECT: RE: HOW DO I GET MYSELF READY TO TALK TO YOU?

Jerry—You're right. There are a few things that you could do that would make our times together more productive, and certainly more satisfying!

First, it's important to make sure our relationship is solid! It's also important to come with the right attitudes. Be willing to be honest, but also be willing to hear Me!

The condition of our relationship actually sets the tone and sets some guidelines for how we're going to interact! Our relationship is the basis for our conversation. Make sure you know where you and I stand, and then tell Me what's on your heart. You can have a plan for your prayer, or, you can just talk to Me. If our relationship is right, I'll be listening!

Principle: You can't just crash Heaven's gates. Prayer requires a prepared heart, and a proper relationship—both toward God—and toward your Christian brothers and sisters. Your heart attitude, or 'heart-itude' is more important than anything else when you pray!

It's important to know how to pray, and proper preparation is the key!

A RIGHT RELATIONSHIP

To speak to the Father is the privilege given only to a child of God. As God's child, you have the privilege—not only to *approach* God—but also to approach His throne *boldly* (Ephesians 3:12; Hebrews 4:14) in full *assurance* that He will hear (Hebrews 10:22). Imagine being able to call the God of all creation 'Daddy' (Romans 8:15; Galatians 4:6)! Proper prayer recognizes that *relationship* as the most important factor (Psalm 34:15). God is only obligated to hear the prayers of His children (Proverbs 15:29; John 9:31; 15:7), and it is to *their* prayers that His 'ears are open' (I Peter 3:12). As the perfect Father, God is never too busy to *listen* to you, to *care* about you, and to *hear* your prayers.

A PREPARED HEART

Once your relationship with God is settled, it's best to begin with a prepared heart (Job 11:13-15). This might be called heart attitude, or 'heart-itude'. That is, a heart that is in tune with God and His will. Even the finest instrument must be tuned before it can be played. So too, must your heart be in tune with God before He can answer your prayers. How do you cultivate a proper heart-itude?

First, be sure you have a *forgiving* heart (Matthew 5:23; 18:21-22; James 5:16). A forgiving heart is a heart which has done its best to be at peace with *others*—even with an enemy (cp. Romans 12:18). To be at peace with others is to be in tune with *God*. While not everyone may choose to forgive *us*, we should pray to forgive others. Jesus instructed us to forgive—and ask forgiveness—*before* we pray (Mark 11:25). If you find it hard to forgive, ask God to *help* you forgive, and try being at peace with everyone the best you are able.

Second, be sure you have a *loving* heart toward your fellow Christians. While you may not always agree with everything they do, you must love your Christian brothers and sisters as Christ loves you (John 13:34; 15:12). Remember, the measure of your love for God is the measure of your love for that fellow-believer you love *least* (I John 4:11; Matthew 7:2; cp. Proverbs 21:13), and we're all in this together (I Corinthians 12:26).

Third, be sure you have a *confessing* heart (I Kings 8:33; Daniel 9:4-11, 20). That is, a heart which recognizes its own sinfulness apart from Christ. A confessing heart calls sin what it is—*sin,* and sees it as God sees it (cp. I Timothy 1:15; see also Psalms 32 and 51). Unconfessed sin can affect your prayer life. Someone has said 'sin will either separate you from prayer, or prayer will separate you from sin' (Psalm 66:18). A confessing heart may *fall* on God's grace when sin occurs, but does not *lean* on God's grace through harboring 'pet sins' or by labeling them 'personal weaknesses' (I John 1:9). Such sins are "…little foxes that spoil the vine" (Song of Solomon 2:15). Confess your sins to God. He knew them when He saved you, and confession clears the way for prayer.

Fourth, be sure you come with a *humble* heart (James 4:6). God hates pride (Proverbs 6:16-17). Pride is seeing yourself or your accomplishments as more important than they are, and can hinder your prayers (Psalm 10:4; Hosea 7:10). God honors humility as long as it is sincere (Colossians 2:18-23). God listens to the prayers of the humble heart (Psalm 9:12; Isaiah 10:17), but hates false humility (cp. Ahaz in Isaiah 7:10-14). Don't try to bluff God with false humility.

Finally, be sure you come with an *obedient* heart. That is, a heart striving to live and submit according to God's will (John 15:7). Even Jesus prayed such (Luke 22:42), and taught us to pray this way (Matthew 6:10). Striving to live according to God's will assumes you *know* God's will expressed in His Word. Study the Word (II Timothy 2:15) to know God's will. He hasn't hidden it—if you *really* want to know it (John 7:17). To align your will with God's will is to guarantee answered prayer (I John 5:14; cp. I John 3:22).

AN APPROPRIATE PLACE

Just as there is no one *posture* that is more acceptable to God (except the posture of your heart), neither is there one acceptable *place* to pray (as was the temple in ancient Jerusalem). But even in the Old Testament, God didn't seem to care where people prayed. He even heard Jonah from the belly of a fish! However, just as a sanctified ('set apart') *heart* is pleasing to God, so too may be a sanctified *place* where you regularly go to meet with Him (cp. Acts 10:9). Personally, I have a small 'prayer closet' (cp. Matthew 6:6; Daniel 6:10) where I pray often. As a sanctified heart is reserved for God alone, so I reserve my prayer closet. In there, I can kneel, weep, praise, and glorify God. While a sanctified place is not necessary, mine is special to me. It is a place of focus where I meet—early and late—with God alone. Remember though, it's not *where* you seek God, but *how* you seek Him (Proverbs 8:17).

My Blog!

The proper posture of the heart, mind, and body make us more ready to really communicate with God. Once the relationship is solid, the mind is aligned with God's wishes, and the body is focused on prayer, our time with God will be the most effective and satisfying part of our day!

Heavenly Homework!

4me2cnsdr.now—

- Do you have a special place where you go to meet with God?

- Do you generally pray with an attitude of 'Thy will be done' or 'my will be done' when you approach God?

- Do you have any 'pet sins' you're harboring that need to be cleared up between you and God?

- Is there someone you need to forgive right now in order to clear the way for the prayers you make to God?

- Is there someone who is upset with you right now that you could ask for forgiveness?

- Is there someone you could pray for that you know will *not* be praying for you?

To do—

- ✓ Make sure prayer is the first and last thing you do each day. Then, fill in the gaps.

✓ In your daily prayers, set apart a special place for your time with God. Be sure you are right with Him, and ask Him to help you forgive others, as He has forgiven you.

Instant Message Summary:

Keep in mind your communication with God rests upon your relationship with Christ. Accept Christ into your heart as your Lord and Savior *first*. Then, your prayers to God are guaranteed to be heard!

CHAPTER 3

"FAITH & FOUNDATION: THE GROUND ZERO OF PRAYER"
BASED ON A PROMISE OR PRINCIPLE

FROM: JERRY
TO: GOD
SUBJECT: WHAT MUST *I* BASE EVERY PRAYER ON?

Ok, God. I've prayed and I'm not getting what I'm asking for! Is there a trick to this? Is there something else I should know before I pray? What am I doing wrong?

FROM: GOD
TO: JERRY
CC: THE CHURCH
SUBJECT: WHAT MUST *I* BASE EVERY PRAYER ON?

Jerry—I AM answering you! Yes, there is something you need to know before sending Me your prayers, but it's not some trick, magic code, or formula! What I want you to know is clearly spelled out in your Bible! It's the instruction book for everything. Please read it.

Principle: You can't just expect God to answer every prayer the way you want Him to. Your requests must be based on a *principle*—or a *universal promise*—expressed in Scripture. This assumes you know His Word, and assures that when God does answer, the answer will align with His perfect will.

FAITH: DIRECTION, NOT AMOUNT!

In praying to God, one of the first things we learn is that we must have *faith* in order to get answers to our prayers. Someone has said: 'faith is putting all your eggs in God's basket, and counting your blessings before they hatch'. Have you ever felt you needed to 'work up' faith in order to please God, or get Him to answer? You don't. The *amount* of faith you have is not important (Matthew 17:20). Remember, if you bring enough faith to pray at all, God can *increase* it! The *fact* of your faith is more important than the *fullness* of your faith (Mark 4:24). What's important is the *object* of your faith (what you lock your faith into)—God! Think of two men standing on an iced over lake. The ice begins to break. Both men are about to sink into the frigid waters. One man has a great deal of faith that the melting ice below his feet will hold him as he crosses the ice to safety. The second man has only a small amount of faith that grasping a rope thrown to him by a friend standing on the frozen shore will actually keep him from drowning. Which man is most likely to survive? You see, it's the *object* of their faith (the ice or the rope) which is important, not the *amount* of faith. Much faith in the wrong thing profits absolutely nothing. Or, think of it this way, does it matter how strong the cord to your electrical appliance is if it's not plugged into a working outlet? Remember—it's the *direction* and the *connection*—not the amount or type—of your faith that pleases God.

FAITH: ALIGNED WITH GOD WILL

Faith must also be in accordance with God's will. It is God alone who knows and does everything right (Philippians 2:13), and it is *alignment* with that perfect will which gets your prayers answered. You cannot simply ask God for anything and think because you *believe*, it will come to pass. You must know and align with God's will, and place the will of God above your own desires (I John 5:14). Even Jesus prayed this way (Matthew 26:39). Only when *you seek, know,* and *desire* God's will does He promise that you can 'believe and receive' (Matthew 21:22).

FAITH: BASED ON A SCRIPTURAL PRINCIPLE OR PRECEPT

But how can you know God's will? You know God's will through knowing God's *Word* (cp. Daniel 9:2, 11; Proverbs 28:9). Faith in prayer must be based on a universal *promise* (such as His willingness to save), or a universal *principle* (such as sin resulting in negative consequences). All God's Word is *for* us, but not all God's Word is *to* us. You have to understand this distinction before claiming 'faith'. To not do so is to ask *wrongly* (James 4:2). For example, God's instruction to "Train up a child in the way he should go and when he is old he will not depart from it" (Proverbs 22:6) is a universal truism for *all* of us. Of course, there are exceptions, but this is generally true. But to claim prosperity and health based upon III John 2 is not proper. John was not talking to *us*, in order that we might all be rich and healthy, but to Gaius, as part of a traditional greeting. This is why Paul encourages us to 'rightly divide the Word' (II Timothy 2:15). In the same way, Namaan the Syrian was instructed to go to the Jordan River to be healed of leprosy. That is not an instruction *to* every Christian for healing, but a lesson *for* us regarding obedience. Remember, your faith must be anchored properly (Psalm 119:49, 89). Someone has well said that prayer is the rope tossed from the boat to the rock—not in order to pull the rock to the *boat*, but to pull the boat to the *rock*. Prayer is *not* to get your will done in Heaven, but to get *God's* will done on earth. God's Word is the Rock of our prayers, and faith based on emotion—or any other such foundation—is mere foolishness. Remind God of His Word when you pray (Nehemiah 1:8). He won't mind a bit.

FAITH THAT DOESN'T WAVER

Sometimes we find it difficult to stand upon our faith without doubting, and most certainly, God understands these occasional doubts. But faith that *constantly* wavers is not pleasing to God (James 1:6-7). Again—be sure your faith is anchored to the Rock. Then, ask—not just *believing* God will answer (Matthew 21:22)—but believing He *already has* (Mark 11:24)!

FAITH BASED ON GOD'S PAST ANSWERS

Finally, as you pray, remember how God has answered *past* prayers for you. Let Him know you trust His *past* faithfulness as an assurance of His *future* dependability (Daniel 9:15-16; cp. II Chronicles 17:16-22). Too often today, we forget God's great answers to our past prayers, and grumble about the small stuff when He delays His answer.

My Blog!

Knowing God's Word will help us pray. By knowing His instructions through His Word, we can know *how* to ask, and *what* to ask for. Putting faith in God's Word and God's will is to anchor ourselves to the only One who can and will protect us through everything. If our faith is right, so will be our prayers.

Heavenly Homework!

4me2cnsdr.now—

- Do you *really* want to know God's will? Why?

- Do you know *enough* of God's Word to remind Him of His promises and principles?

- In prayer, what's the difference between working *with* your faith and working *up* your faith?

To do—

- ✓ If you find you don't always have enough faith, or if you feel your faith is wavering, spend time reading God's Word, and ask Him to help your faith to grow. (See Mark 9:24!) Keep in mind, growth is not always a quick or easy process, but to know and grow in Christ is the most important part of your Christian growth.

- ✓ Study God's Word—His principles and promises—to learn His will.

- ✓ Develop an attitude of drawing your prayers toward *God's* will rather than trying to bend God's ear toward what *you* really want.

Instant Message Summary:

In knowing God's Word, you will learn His character, His will, and be more able to pray effectively.

CHAPTER 4

"EXAMPLES OF PRAYER"
MODELS FOR THE AGES!

FROM: JERRY
TO: GOD
SUBJECT: CAN YOU SHOW ME WHAT AN EFFECTIVE PRAYER LOOKS LIKE?

God—I think I am getting it, but there's so much to read in the Bible! Is there anywhere I can look that might show me what a really good prayer should look like?

FROM: GOD
TO: JERRY
CC: THE CHURCH
SUBJECT: CAN YOU SHOW ME WHAT AN EFFECTIVE PRAYER LOOKS LIKE?

Jerry—Thanks for asking! Yes, there are several wonderful prayers in the Bible! The prayers of Jesus, Daniel, Hezekiah and many others are in there! Read them, and discover what I find pleasing in them.

Principle: God has given you models for prayer through the prayers of some of the great men of Scripture. In these prayers, you will find what God desires in the prayers you pray! Study them carefully.

THE PRAYERS OF JESUS

Who could be a better example in prayer than Christ? While His prayer in Matthew 6:9-13 is called the 'Lord's Prayer', it is not. It is an *example* of prayer given us by the Lord. The *real* Lord's Prayer is in John 17. Study both prayers. Note how Christ acknowledges: the *holiness* and *uniqueness* of God, *God's* will and glory as the primary emphasis, the *specificity* of His requests, and the importance of *obedience* to God and His Word.

THE PRAYER OF DANIEL

The prayer of Daniel 9:1-19 is another of the great prayers in the Bible. Look closely at how the prophet emphasizes: praise *before* petition, *self-denial,* understanding God's *mercy* and *righteousness,* the reasons He sometimes disciplines us, *confession* of sin, and trusting God's *character* to answer the right way.

THE PRAYER OF HEZEKIAH

Hezekiah and his people were in serious trouble from a foreign invader when he offered this majestic prayer in II Kings 19. See how the king approached God in genuine *repentance,* emphasized God's greatness and honor *above* the importance of his request, and understood that *God's glory in the eyes of the world* was what mattered most.

THE PRAYER OF PAUL

Paul was one of the greatest of all the apostles. Study his prayer to God in Ephesians 3:14-21. See how Paul recognized the *richness* out of which God delights in blessing us, as well as the importance of *Christ,* and His *love* and *glory.* Note too, that glory to Father and Son is the *most* important thing to Paul in his prayer.

THE PRAYER OF EZRA

Ezra was an Old Testament priest at the time of the rebuilding of the temple in Jerusalem. Recognizing the sinfulness of the people, Ezra prayed. Study in Ezra 9:6-15 how the prophet: acknowledges sin *before* asking favor, praises God for what He's *already* done, and recognizes the *goodness* and *mercy* of God in not punishing as much as He *could* have. Note how Ezra stresses his own complete *unworthiness.*

THE PRAYERS OF DAVID

David was perhaps Israel's greatest king. Note in II Samuel 7:18-29 how he stresses his own *humility,* God's *Word,* God's *greatness,* and God's *faithfulness.* Again, in I

Chronicles 17:16-27, note how David emphasizes his humility, and God's *will, power, redemption* and *glory*. David recalls God's *past* blessings, which assure him of God's *future* faithfulness, and bases his own requests on God's *Word* and *promises*.

THE PRAYER OF JEREMIAH

Jeremiah was a prophet in Israel whose message was virtually ignored. Notice how he extols God as *Creator*, and the *concern, redemption*, and *blessing* of God regarding His people (Jeremiah 32:16-25).

THE PRAYER OF SOLOMON

Solomon was the wealthiest of all the kings of Judah. Read his prayer at the dedication of the first temple in Jerusalem (I Kings 8:22-61). Do you see how Solomon recognizes God's *future faithfulness* based on *past blessings?* Notice how he stresses the *smallness* of man compared to the *greatness* of God, the importance of *glorifying God to outsiders*, and his own trust in God's *righteousness, forgiveness, and sovereignty*. Don't miss how Solomon: begins with *praise* and *thanksgiving*, and emphasizes that God *alone* can deal with sinful hearts.

In all these prayers, did you notice that the *personal* requests were less emphasized than God's *holiness, goodness*, and *will?* Try not to make these model prayers formula-prayers, but remember what you may learn from them.

My Blog!

By studying the prayers of others, which God finds pleasing, we can learn more about Him and what He's looking for. Remember, in all these prayers, some of the personality and thoughts of the person praying were present. God doesn't want cookie-cutter prayers. He wants us to be personal with Him, and to grow and mature in our prayers.

Heavenly Homework!

4me2cnsdr.now—

- What do all the model prayers have in common?

- What is the general *order* in these prayers?

- Which of the model prayers do you relate to most? Why?

- What is generally the first thing you pray for, or about, when you pray?

- How might you be able to glorify God in the eyes of the world?

- What *past* answers to prayers can you recall that assure you of God's faithfulness in answering your *future* prayers?

To do—

- ✓ Choose one of the model prayers in this chapter and make a list of the key points of emphasis. Use those in your own prayer today. Try this several times with different model prayers. See if it makes a difference.

- ✓ Look at the prayer of Ezra in Ezra 9:6. How does *your* approach to God compare?

- ✓ Look at Isaiah's approach to God in Isaiah 6:15. How does *your* approach to God compare?

- ✓ Look at the prayer of the Levites in Nehemiah 9:4-37. Study and analyze it. What stands out?

- ✓ When you pray, try visualizing yourself as God might have seen you *before* you were saved. Remember, while you approach God as His child, you should come in the humility of a sinner saved by grace.

Instant Message Summary:

The model prayers of Scripture show us that prayer does not have a set format. They do show that effective prayer does recognize God's holiness, His righteousness, and His mercy. Make sure your prayers recognize them too, and aren't just lists of requests.

CHAPTER 5

"HOW TO—AND NOT TO—PRAY"
CAUTIONS ALONG THE WAY

FROM: JERRY
TO: GOD
SUBJECT: ARE THERE SOME SPECIAL RIGHT AND WRONG WAYS TO TALK TO YOU?

Thanks, God! Those model prayers really helped! But all those people lived a long time ago, and a lot of the prayers I hear in church or on TV are different from the way I pray. Are there right and wrong ways to talk to You?

FROM: GOD
TO: JERRY
CC: THE CHURCH
SUBJECT: ARE THERE SOME SPECIAL RIGHT AND WRONG WAYS TO TALK TO YOU?

Jerry—there's not really a right or wrong way, but there are some things to keep in mind so you aren't wasting your time or Mine! Be sure to remember that prayer from your heart is the most pleasing prayer. I care little for grandly constructed prayers crafted with fancy speech. Keep it simple, be specific, and tell Me what's on your heart.

Principle: While there is no set formula for prayer, there are some ways in which people pray that are either inappropriate and/or misunderstood. Be sure you take advantage of every acceptable way to talk to God without wasting either His time—or yours.

THE SIMPLICITY OF PRAYER

Have you ever heard someone pray a great 'swelling' prayer in King James English? Did you think God must have heard them because of this? God may have heard them, but not because of the 'greatness' of the prayer. God wants you to come to Him in *simplicity* and *honesty*, and He promises not to rebuke you. For example, Jonah was upset with God, and told Him so (Jonah 4:1-11). God still heard him. When you pray, simple and honest is more important than long and 'flowery'.

THE SPECIFICITY OF PRAYER

"God, bless the world and all the people in it." Some prayers are so general that the one praying might never know if their requests are answered! God knows your needs even before you ask (Isaiah 65:24; cp. Daniel 9:20-23). You do not need to impress Him with blanket requests—hoping that at least some things in them will be answered. I used to pray blanket prayers so God wouldn't be disappointed if He couldn't answer specific requests! But *blanket* prayers don't allow for *specific* praise! Never think anything is too big or too small for God to answer. After all, what could be 'big' to God? Be as specific in your prayers as Jesus was (Matthew 6:11; cp. James 4:2), and glorify God—whatever His answer! When you are specific in your prayers, you can glorify Him for *specific* answers to *specific* requests.

THE STRENGTH OF PRAYER

While one type of prayer may not be more important than another to God, the prayer of *unity*—believers praying with other believers—is certainly a powerful type of prayer. Exactly *why* this is so is not clear, but Jesus emphasized the practice in Matthew 18:19. Pray, and *agree* in prayer, with fellow Christians. It could just be that there is a 'multiplication factor' in the added prayer of a partner (cp. Deuteronomy 32:30), or in the collective prayers of a nation. And while we're discussing powerful prayers, although it cannot be proved by Scripture, it is my personal opinion that the prayers of a child are especially touching to God's heart (cp. Matthew 18:10). Perhaps it is because the little ones have more recently been in His presence.

PRAYER IS NOT A FORMULA

Prayer is not a mantra to be recited to God. There is no set 'formula' which God requires. As long as your prayer is *sincere*, directed toward *God's* glory, grounded in *faith,* and wrapped in *trust*—God will hear you. In teaching young people what to pray for, I suggest a simple but effective memory tool. I have them spread out and look at the five fingers of one hand. The *pointing* finger reminds them to pray for those who point the way, such as teachers, youth ministers, etc. The *tallest* finger reminds them to pray for those in high positions in the world, such as presidents and other leaders. The *weakest* finger reminds them to pray for those who are ill, or those, such as little children and pets, who are *unable* to pray. The *little* finger is the most distant, and reminds them to pray for those who are traveling, far away, or are on the missionary fields. The *thumb* is for those closest to them, such as family and friends. All five fingers form a fist. This reminds them to pray for those who are enemies—to them, to their family, or to their country. However you pray, know that prayer is *personal*. Mechanical prayers mean nothing to God. "God is great, God is good…" is a fine model for children, but not for you.

PRAYER IS NOT EMPTY REPETITION

Have you ever heard prayers where the same requests were made over and over and *over*—as if God might have missed them at the first mention? Jesus chastised the Pharisees for such (Matthew 6:7). Someone has said: 'painted prayers are lifeless, and frozen prayers never rise'. Take care that your mind doesn't drift as you pray, and that your prayer doesn't become a broken record (Job 35:13). Every prayer should be fresh, from a trusting heart, never forced or routine. God surely frowns upon those who have much more to say in public prayers than in private ones.

PRAYER IS NOT IN UNKNOWN TONGUES

For many years I was taught that I needed to learn a 'prayer language', based on I Corinthians 14:14-16. Eventually, I thought I received this 'gift', and was able to pray in an 'unknown tongue' having no idea what I was saying. I began to wonder, though, if God heard this language in a more special way than He heard my 'regular' prayers, how would He hear the prayers of deaf mutes at all? God understands *all* languages. Better still, it's your *heart*—not your *lips*—that He listens to. That's why we can sometimes pray silently, or still pray when we simply don't know what to say. The 'language' of your heart is the *real* prayer language, and sometimes words just get in the way.

PRAYER IS NOT MEASURED BY LENGTH

It is more important how *often* you pray than how *long* your prayers are. The shortest prayer in the Bible saved a drowning man! Peter's prayer was only three words (Matthew 14:30; cp. Matthew 8:25; 9:27), and Jesus answered (cp. Luke 18:13)! Tell God what's on your heart, and move on.

PRAYER DOES NOT LOOK FOR A SIGN

Sometimes we really want 'proof' that God has heard, and will answer our prayers. It's just human nature. In the Old Testament, Gideon wanted such proof, and put out a fleece of wool, asking God to show—through the dew upon the fleece—that He would answer Gideon's prayer. God answered. Based on this example, I remember being told that I should 'put out my fleece' when I prayed, and *test* God to show me a sign that He was going to answer. Because Gideon put out a fleece, however, is not a reason to do the same. How much better to *trust* God through faith than to require a sign. All too often, faith looking for a sign is nothing more than doubt looking for proof. Remember, all Scripture is *for* us, not all Scripture is *to* us (Chapter 3).

PRAYER IS NOT 'NAME IT AND CLAIM IT'

Despite some teaching to the contrary, we should *never* attempt to control God, as we would a puppet, through ritual and self will. We do not tell the holy, righteous, God of the universe and eternity *what* He must do, and how He *must* answer our prayers. Neither is God *obligated* to give us what we 'claim' in faith. To 'claim' for ourselves something we think should be ours is to put ourselves—and our will—ahead of God's ultimate plan. *That* is presumption (Chapter 10). *That* is asking 'amiss' (James 4:2-3). I recall when my mother was sick with cancer. I 'claimed' Isaiah 53:5 "…with His stripes we are healed." My mother died. Only later did I understand that the passage was true as a universal promise for *salvation*, not physical healing. *All* who seek salvation, receive (Isaiah 45:22). But *not* everyone (including my mother) is *physically* healed. When you pray, only 'claim' what you *know* God has promised to you in Scripture, not what you *think* you want or need through (so-called) faith. Seek God's will above your own, and His glory above your desires.

PRAYER: BE CAREFUL WHAT YOU ASK FOR

King Hezekiah became ill, and it was time for him to die. He begged God to lengthen his life (Isaiah 38:1-5). God did, and Hezekiah had a son, Manasseh. Manasseh grew up to become one of the worst kings in Israel's history (II Kings 23:26). In like manner, the Hebrews who escaped Egypt at the Exodus tired of God's manna as food, and begged for meat. God answered their request, but it 'brought leanness to their souls' (Psalm 106:15). Sometimes we pray *unwisely* and God gives us the desires of our heart. Later, we learn submission to God the hard way. Be careful what you ask God for. It is better to ask for what you know *is* His will than to beg for what you're *not sure* is. Study His Word, and trust His will. He knows what's best for you.

My Blog!

Prayer is a powerful thing! But God doesn't want showy or repetitious prayers. He doesn't mind if we pray about the same things daily, but we need to remember to think about what we're praying for, not just pray using a formula or flowery phrases. We should talk to God with our minds and hearts, not with fancy or formulaic speech.

Heavenly Homework!

4me2cnsdr.now—

- Do you try not to let God know when you're upset?

- Why might the prayers of a child be so tender to the heart of God?

- What's the difference between a *childlike* prayer and a *childish* prayer?

- Do you find yourself repeating the same 'formula' in your prayers? How can you change this?

- How do you go about remembering what you want to pray for?

- What, in faith, are you *totally* trusting God for at this point in your life?

- Are there some things you have been trying to talk God into?

- Why do so many people seek miracles and signs from God?

To do—

- ✓ Look at how Solomon presents his requests to God in Proverbs 30:5-9. Make a list of some of the characteristics in that prayer which would be good to remember. Use those characteristics in your own prayers today.

- ✓ When you pray, try telling God how you *really* feel.

✓ Try praying without saying a word—let your heart speak to God.

✓ Try praying *with* others. Remember, you do not need to impress them or God with your prayers.

✓ Pray for the peace of Jerusalem (Psalm 122:6).

✓ Pray for America (II Chronicles 7:14).

Instant Message Summary:

Prayer is personal communion with God. He hears our real thoughts and feelings, and is not impressed with carefully constructed speeches or mindless rote formulas.

Remember, when you pray, make sure you pray from your heart, and 'tell it like it is' to God.

CHAPTER 6

"THE FEET OF PRAYER"
DOING WHAT YOU CAN, OR BECOMING YOUR OWN ANSWER

FROM: JERRY
TO: GOD
SUBJECT: SHOULD I PRAY FOR THINGS I CAN DO MYSELF?

OK, God. I think I understand a little better how to pray, and why prayer is important. But I'm having trouble determining just what to pray for. You've made it clear that you aren't just some big Santa Claus who exists to meet my every whim and desire. So, should I pray only when I need help? And should I pray about some of the things I can do for myself?

FROM: GOD
TO: JERRY
CC: THE CHURCH
SUBJECT: SHOULD I PRAY FOR THINGS I CAN DO MYSELF?

Jerry—You're right! I'm not Santa Claus, and I have enabled you to do some things yourself. Sometimes in life, you must put feet to your faith and be the answer to your own prayers! Because you're praying to Me about the problem, you're allowing Me to be glorified for the answer. But after you pray, get up and see if you can become part of My answer. In using you to become the answer to your own prayers, I show that I can work through the weakness of man as well as through the miraculous things of the world.

Principle: God loves to answer your prayers. But sometimes we pray for the very things we can do ourselves. While we must fall upon His grace and mercy to do what we can't, when we are able, God expects us to be the answer to our own prayers, and be the instrument of His will.

DOING *WHAT* YOU ARE ABLE IS MORE PLEASING TO GOD THAN HOW *MUCH* YOU ARE ABLE TO DO.

When you pray, the first question you should ask yourself when you finish is: "Can I be the answer to anything I just prayed about?" As Isaiah learned when he prayed concerning his nation's need for a prophet—sometimes the person praying can be the answer to his own prayer (Isaiah 6:8-9). Just as God gave Isaiah the gifts and abilities to be the answer to his own prayer, so God has given you some unique gifts and abilities as well. Even if you cannot be the *ultimate* answer to your prayer, God expects you to do your part. You might be a partial answer (cp. Acts 9:6).

Someone has said: "God will direct your arrows, but expects you to string your own bow."

I recall when a teacher friend was diagnosed with cancer at the school where I taught. She was forced to take off a number of weeks for treatment. As I prayed that God would heal her, and provide for her during her time off, the request was made at our school for teachers to donate sick days to her in order to lessen the financial strain the sickness was causing. I realized that in being able to do this, I could be at least a *partial* answer to my own prayer! In donating a sick day, my involvement didn't *diminish* God's provision, it gave God an opportunity to work through me, and strengthen my faith as well. Pray for a good garden, then pick up the hoe!

EVEN WHEN GOD PLANS AND REVEALS HIS WILL, HE EXPECTS US TO ACT WHEN WE CAN TO SET THAT WILL IN MOTION.

While God is all-powerful, and we can be sure His perfect will is going to take place in the end, remember—doing what you are able to help *fulfill* God's will is *also* a part of His plan. Someone might respond: 'If God is going to have His way, why should we even pray?' The response? It may be that God's way is to answer *through* our prayer (cp. II Peter 1:10). God's work through our prayers is certainly not the *only* way He performs His will, but He has planned that it is certainly *one* of them. For example, where the issue of God healing the sick is mentioned in Scripture, God expected those involved to not only *pray*—but to also *do*—what they were able (James 5:14; cp. Isaiah 38:21; see also Mark 14:8). Too, when God directed Joseph to provide grain for all Egypt and Canaan during the famine, Joseph's brothers—and all the people—were still required to come *get* the grain. God did not send it to them. In the same way, we know that God alone is in charge of saving souls, but He has chosen to do this partly though *our* witness. As such, we become an instrument of His will. (See Chapter 10.) Remember, when you pray, do what you can, and trust God to take care of the rest.

My Blog!

Our job as believers is to pray to God *in* and *for* all things. We are to trust Him to perform His perfect will in everything, but we are also to be willing agents for bringing about His answers. We are to put 'feet to our faith'.

Heavenly Homework!

4me2cnsdr.now—

- Is there anything you are praying for that you could do *yourself* right now?

- How is God using you right now in the lives of others?

To do—

- ✓ Write down your prayers for a week. Each day, look over what you've prayed about, and ask yourself, "What can *I* do to help answer these prayers?" Choose at least one prayer per day and be sure you do all you can to 'help' God answer it. Then, give God the glory for the answers He has provided!

Instant Message Summary:

Be sure to pray in *all* things, and keep your heart open to the stirrings of the Holy Spirit. You might be the answer to your own prayers.

CHAPTER 7

"INTERCESSORY PRAYER"
STANDING IN THE GAP

FROM: JERRY
TO: GOD
SUBJECT: CAN SOMEONE PRAY IN PLACE OF SOMEONE ELSE?

I have a dilemma, God. I heard someone mention they were 'standing in the gap' for another person. What does that mean? Is it something I should be doing as well?

FROM: GOD
TO: JERRY
CC: THE CHURCH
SUBJECT: CAN SOMEONE PRAY IN PLACE OF SOMEONE ELSE?

Jerry—When someone 'stands in the gap' for another, it means they are filling the prayer place for that person. You can pray for others or in place of others. Praying for them means you are concerned about them and are bringing your concerns to Me. Praying in place of another means you are praying because they can't or won't pray. Both are pleasing prayers to Me.

Principle: People praying for things are not the only prayers God listens to. Intercessory prayer—praying for, or in place of another—is also an important aspect of prayer. Jesus is praying for you and me before the Father, and so is God's Holy Spirit! Someone praying for someone else is called 'intercession', and when you intercede for others, it can become one of the most powerful prayers you can offer.

YOUR PRAYER FOR OTHERS

To *intercede* means 'to stand in place of, or to rescue, another'. When you pray for someone else, you are interceding before God for them (cp. Moses for Israel in Exodus 32:11-34). Intercessory prayer is not only a privilege, but can be one of the most powerful types of prayers you can pray. Why? Because intercession is *selfless* prayer. It is prayer that takes you away from *personal* concerns, and brings before God your concern for *others*. God spared an entire city because of the intercessory prayer of one man (Genesis 19:21, 29)!

But there is another reason intercessory prayer is powerful prayer. Sometimes, through unforeseen or difficult circumstances, God gives you an opportunity to pray for someone you might *never* pray for otherwise. For example, Abraham unwisely journeyed to Egypt during a famine. While there, he nearly lost Sarah, his wife, to the pharaoh Abimelech. While God did not *condone* Abraham's situation, it did give Abraham opportunity to pray for a man he would *never* have prayed for, and in the end, the Pharaoh was blessed (Genesis 20:17).

God instructs us to pray for each other. It is not an option, but a necessity in your Christian growth (Colossians 1:3; cp. Philippians 1:3). Failing to pray for others is called 'sin against the Lord' (I Samuel 12:23). Take time out from making personal requests to God, and intercede for others. After all, others are interceding for you!

CHRIST'S PRAYER FOR YOU

Intercessory prayer is not only you praying for *others*, but also Christ, in Heaven, praying for *you* (Romans 8:34; I John 2:1). He is your heavenly attorney before the Father, fending off every charge old Satan brings against you (Job 1:6-9). Because Christ came as God in the flesh, He can be your *'kinsman redeemer'* in Heaven (Leviticus 25:49). Christ is the *'daysman'* Job so wished for in his time of trouble (Job 9:33). In the story of Sodom and Gomorrah, God spared Lot because of the prayers of another—his uncle Abraham (Genesis 18:16-32). As Lot was 'in Abraham' (in concern and prayer), so we are 'in Christ'. Never forget—while Jesus died to save you (John 3:16), He now lives before God as your great High Priest in Heaven *keeping* you saved (Hebrews 7:24-25; 9:24). As you pray for others in the 'name of Jesus' (see Chapter 12), Jesus prays in His own name for you before the Father. (See I Timothy 2:5; John 17).

THE HOLY SPIRIT'S PRAYER FOR YOU

Did you know that not only Christ, but also God's Holy Spirit, prays for you before the Father? Have you ever experienced times when you simply did not know how to pray for someone or something? At such times, we are told that the Spirit *within* us intercedes *for* us to the Father. The Spirit reads our hearts and signs our prayers in handwriting always recognized by God (Romans 8:22; 26-27; cp. Galatians 4:6; Ephesians 6:18; Jude 20; cp. John 4:22-24). This is prayer without saying a word. It is the 'soundless sigh' of the *Holy Spirit* groaning *for* us—not through us. It is not a 'prayer language' in an unknown tongue, but the Spirit speaking in the tongue of perfect communication with God in a language which *cannot* be spoken (see Chapter 5). As the great preacher Charles Spurgeon once noted: "...spiritual groans that cannot be uttered are generally prayers that cannot be denied". Why? Because God's Spirit knows even the *intent* of your prayer (I Chronicles 28:9). Remember though, this isn't a type of prayer to *lean* on when you simply don't feel like praying, but prayer you can *fall back* on when you don't know how to put your prayer into words (I Corinthians 14:15).

My Blog!

By praying for others, we show we care about them, and trust God to do what is right for them. This will bring glory to God, and open an avenue for answered prayer! God honors our prayers for others, and we should be diligent in our efforts, especially in praying for the salvation of others. The Holy Spirit prays *for* us, and *through* us. We should intercede for others as well.

Heavenly Homework!

4me2cnsdr.now—

- Is there someone special you are interceding for when you pray?

- Who are you fairly sure intercedes for *you* when *they* pray?

- Can you recall a time when intercession was very effective in your prayer?

- Who in the world might you be least likely to intercede for in prayer? Why?

- Is intercessory prayer (for you) more of a *burden*, an *obligation*, or a *privilege?*

- Do you intercede for world leaders?

- What is Jesus interceding for *you* about before the Father?

- Can you recall a time when you simply did not know how you should pray? What did you do?

- Why do you think God doesn't need to hear our prayers in an unknown 'prayer language'?

To do—

- ✓ Choose one person you know who may not pray as often as they should, or may not be Christian. Pray for them daily! Watch how the Lord works in their life, and how He works in yours *through* these prayers.

Instant Message Summary:

Praying for others is not only acceptable to God, but recommended! Intercessory prayer is especially pleasing to God. Pray for others on earth as you are being prayed for in Heaven.

CHAPTER 8

"THE SACRIFICE OF PRAYER"
PRAYER THAT COSTS

FROM: JERRY
TO: GOD
SUBJECT: WHAT IF I JUST DON'T FEEL LIKE PRAYING?

God, I'll be honest. This prayer stuff is sometimes just not what I want to do! When I'm discouraged, or hurt, or even disillusioned with it all, I don't want to talk to You. Is it wrong if I just don't feel like praying?

FROM: GOD
TO: JERRY
CC: THE CHURCH
SUBJECT: WHAT IF I JUST DON'T FEEL LIKE PRAYING?

Jerry—I know you don't always want to pray! I know all of your thoughts! But the prayers you do pray when you're discouraged or disillusioned are even more special to Me! Please keep praying!

Principle: We're all human. Sometimes you are tired, frustrated, disappointed, or just plain hurting. Sometimes life deals you a blow and you just don't feel like praying. Prayers at such times touch the heart of God in a special way.

PRAYER WHEN YOU HURT

Sacrifice was the foundation for pleasing God in the Old Testament. We are called on to sacrifice as well. A sacrifice is something that *costs* us to give to God, but something we do because we know it pleases Him. Prayer when you hurt is a prayer of sacrifice, and must be very special to God (cp. Hebrews 13:15). The ancient Greeks loved to tell the story of Menthe. Menthe loved Hades, lord of the underworld. But Hades could not return this affection. Hades loved Persephone, daughter of Demeter, goddess of grain. Eventually, Persephone began to resent the affection Menthe showed Hades and vowed to destroy her. Persephone trampled Menthe under her feet. In dying, Menthe forgave Persephone and released before her a most beautiful fragrance. Appreciating such forgiveness, Hades transformed Menthe into an herb—mint, which can only release its most precious fragrance when it has been crushed. Such is the nature of sacrificial prayer. Prayer offered to God when your spirit is crushed. I recall praying for over a year for my mother to be healed of cancer. The night she died, it was hard to pray. God had answered, but His answer was 'no', and that wasn't what I'd been trusting Him for. I wasn't sure how to approach God in prayer that night, but I understood that to be able to praise Him for what I couldn't understand at this moment might be a 'sacrifice of praise' opportunity I might never get again. Never forget to praise God—especially when He allows the 'bread of adversity' to become your occasional meal. His heart may be especially touched by such prayers (cp. Psalm 18:6; 106:44; Hebrews 5:7-8, and Isaiah 30:19-20).

PRAYER WHEN YOU'RE FASTING

There are times when the sacrifice of prayer is physical and voluntary (Daniel 9:3). How fasting specifically affects our prayers, we aren't told. Nevertheless, Scripture does sanction it (cp. Matthew 6:16; I Corinthians 7:5; II Corinthians 6:5). True fasting is not always easy. When you pray fasting, just be sure you don't desire to be seen doing it, for that becomes your only reward (Matthew 6:18).

PRAYER FOR AN ENEMY

Without a doubt, this type prayer is one of the most difficult, but Jesus said to do it (Matthew 5:44). Kindness toward those who dislike us seems to be especially pleasing to God (cp. Proverbs 25:22; Romans 12:20; II Timothy 4:16). Remember—praying for an enemy is a unique sacrifice, and such an opportunity may glorify God in a special way.

PRAYER WHEN YOU JUST DON'T FEEL LIKE PRAYING

Let's face it, there are times when you just don't feel like praying, and the door for your prayers to Heaven seems like 'iron' (Leviticus 26:19). When those times happen—and they will—prayer really *is* a sacrifice. Just be sure it isn't sin that's keeping you from wanting to pray, and pray anyway! Remember, God doesn't just hear you when you *enjoy* praying, but sometimes He may be especially pleased when you *don't*. At those times it becomes a sacrifice.

PRAYER WHEN GOOD THINGS COME

This might seem strange, but have you ever considered receiving compliments as a *sacrificial* prayer to God? Consider it another opportunity for the 'sacrifice of praise'. When God blesses you—perhaps through compliments you receive from others—don't keep them. Hand these blessings to God and ask Him to place them in His 'praise bank' where He may utilize them for *His* glory as a 'sweet savor' before His throne (cp. Leviticus 2:2; Revelation 5:8; 8:4).

PRAYER WHEN EVIL SEEMS TO BE PRESENT

We live in an evil world. Our battle is against dark forces, and sometimes those forces seem particularly close. When you feel spiritual darkness around you, or when God's Spirit within you seems to be drawn more forcefully toward heaven, *pray*. It could be that God wants you especially close to Him (Ephesians 6:12-18).

My Blog!

Prayers when we don't feel like praying—for people we don't feel like praying *for*, and at *times* when we don't want to pray—are some of the most pleasing prayers to God. They are the prayers that tell Him His wishes are more important than our own.

Heavenly Homework!

4me2cnsdr.now—

- Has there ever been a time when you just didn't *want* to pray? Why was that? What did you do?

- Why do you think fasting is important?

- Who can you pray for today that you would normally *never* pray for?

- Has there ever been a time when Heaven seemed like 'iron' regarding your prayers? What was the reason?

- Is there something happening in your life right now that you might never get another chance to pray about?

To do—

✓ It's very difficult to pray for good things to happen to someone who has genuinely harmed you or hurt you. Make it a habit to pray for such people. Don't make this a prayer of vengeance, but instead, ask God to bless this person as He has never done before. This prayer of sacrifice will please God.

✓ The next time you receive a compliment, lay it on the 'altar' of your place of prayer and offer it to God in love and adoration for all He means to you.

Instant Message Summary:

Prayer isn't always easy or comfortable. Pray anyway.

CHAPTER 9

"*THE PERSEVERANCE OF PRAYER* "
CONTINUING TO KNOCK WHEN THE DOOR SEEMS CLOSED

FROM: JERRY
TO: GOD
SUBJECT: HOW LONG AND HOW OFTEN SHOULD I PRAY WITHOUT SHOWING A LACK OF FAITH?

God, there are some requests I've made that I haven't seemed to get answers for. If I keep praying for these things, does this show that I don't believe you will answer them? Don't you get tired of my continual requests for some of the same things? How should I know when to quit?

FROM: GOD
TO: JERRY
CC: THE CHURCH
SUBJECT: HOW LONG AND HOW OFTEN SHOULD I PRAY WITHOUT SHOWING A LACK OF FAITH?

*Jerry, I'm not offended when you pray for things over and over. That's not what I meant when I said not to pray repetitious prayers. I was talking about mindless repetition of words. Yours are genuine requests, and I always want to hear those! There really isn't a set time to stop praying for something. Sometimes My answer is 'wait a bit', but I know that's difficult for you. Sometimes, what I want is that you **do** keep praying! This shows Me you **do** have faith—not that your faith is weak. So keep right on praying for whatever is in your heart!*

Principle: It is not a lack of faith to keep praying when God hasn't seemed to answer. To keep diligently making requests and pleading before God, in fact, shows greater faith. So does staying in an attitude of prayer at all times.

PRAYER THAT KEEPS ASKING

Do you think God ever gets tired of listening to you? Do you think He ever gets weary of hearing your requests over, and over, and over? No. In fact, God encourages you to *keep* asking, *keep* seeking, and *keep* knocking on Heaven's door. Moses prayed for forty days (Deuteronomy 9:18, 25)! This prayer of determination is called prayer of *importunity*. Importunity means 'persistence', and believe it or not—God delights in such prayer (Matthew 7:7-11)! The problem is not that we ask *too often*. The problem is that we don't ask often *enough* (James 4:2; cp. Colossians 4:2), or we *stop* asking before God stops giving (Genesis 18:23-33; cp. Ephesians 3:20; Jeremiah 33:3)! *Keep* asking God to meet your needs. His supply of blessing is *unlimited* (Ephesians 3:16, 20; Philippians 4:19). Don't think such asking shows a lack or faith, or bothers Him. Prayer that keeps *on* asking is prayer that shows you have faith enough to never give up trusting God (Luke 11:5-13; cp. Luke 18:1-5).

PRAYER THAT STAYS ON THE LINE

Have you ever wondered just how many times a day you should pray? Is ten times enough? Is twenty too many? Actually, you should pray only *once*. What? Pray only once? Yes! As I used to tell my youth group when teaching them prayer: *'Stay on the line, and you won't need a dime!'* Go to God in an *attitude* of prayer and *stay* on the line! Scripture instructs you to 'pray without ceasing' (Ephesians 1:16; I Thessalonians 5:17; cp. Ephesians 6:18). That is, instead of 'phoning' God whenever you need to speak to Him, *stay* on the line with Him, and *remain* in an attitude of prayer through all your waking hours (I Timothy 5:5; Romans 12:12). In this way you will live in the continual leading of God's Spirit in everything you do (Colossians 4:2; Philippians 4:6). Keeping in a constant attitude of prayer is the finest 'life compass' you will ever have (cp. Psalm 55:17; Acts 12:5). Make sure your prayer 'cell phone' is fully charged (cp. Ephesians 5:18), and stay on the line to heaven!

PRAYER THAT IS INTENSE AND DETERMINED

Was there ever a time when you found yourself—not just praying—but on your knees in *deep* and *pleading* prayer from a heart that was heavy with concern (cp. Hebrews 5:7)? All prayer is important, and we should take all our prayers seriously. But sometimes we have a special burden on our hearts, or a prayer issue which seems especially urgent (cp. Nehemiah 8:6). This intense type of prayer isn't more important to God than any other, but it is prayer that intensifies our *expression* and *focus* as we speak to Him (see Daniel 9:3). God says He hears and listens to such diligent prayer (James 5:16-17; Hebrews 11:6; cp. I Thessalonians 3:10). During those times when your heart is especially burdened, remember, God understands, and will recognize, the urgency of your prayer. Go *boldly* before Him (Hebrews 4:16). Pray with all your heart, and God will respond (Jeremiah 29:12-13). Pray with *intensity*. In His righteousness, God will answer (Psalm 143:1).

PRAYER WHEN GOD CALLS YOU TO PRAY

Sometimes, if you're listening, God will call you to meet with Him as He did young Samuel in the temple (I Samuel 3:1-8). As with Samuel, there have been times during the wee hours of the morning—perhaps when I could not sleep—that I felt God calling me to prayer. You may not feel this mysterious call often—and you may not understand the purpose—but when you hear it, know God has a reason. It may be that at that particular time, God wants to work through your prayer alone. Always listen for that special call of God.

My Blog!

Prayer is fellowship with God. Christians can't really get too much of that! God wants us to pray constantly! Stay in touch with God; that's when He can work best!

Heavenly Homework!

4me2cnsdr.now—

- What have you been praying for the *most*, or the *longest?*

- When was the last time you prayed on your face before God?

- When was the last time you wept, on your knees, in prayer?

To do—

- ✓ It's easy to put prayer into a little box, like something you take out and do periodically, but then put away to continue the rest of your day. Try talking to God throughout the day, and keep asking Him for the answers to your requests. He's always listening.

✓ See how Elijah prayed (I Kings 18:42). Why did he pray this way? Have you ever prayed like this?

✓ Note the prayer of David (Psalm 6:6). Have you ever prayed in this way? When? Why?

✓ Practice being in a constant *attitude* of prayer. Note how this affects your daily activities.

Instant Message Summary:

God wants us to keep praying, even when we feel like we've prayed for something a lot! Never tire of praying. Your prayers keep you close to Him, and that brings Him glory.

CHAPTER 10

"THE MOST PLEASING PRAYER"
PRAYER FOR SURE THINGS

FROM: JERRY
TO: GOD
SUBJECT: WHAT ABOUT PRAYING FOR SURE THINGS?

I have another question, God. You tell me in the Bible to pray in all things. Does that mean everything? What about stuff I know is in Your will, and things I'm sure You're going to take care of? Doesn't praying for those almost show a lack of faith?

FROM: GOD
TO: JERRY
CC: THE CHURCH
SUBJECT: WHAT ABOUT PRAYING FOR SURE THINGS?

Yes, Jerry—pray in all things, about everything. Praying for the things that seem certain show Me that you have placed your trust in Me for everything, and that you aren't presuming on My grace or mercy. You offer Me an opportunity to bless you, and you become closer to Me through your prayers.

Principle: The most pleasing prayer to God is the prayer that totally eliminates pride and presumption, and shows total reliance on God. Pray—even for things that seem certain—so that you can glorify God for His provision when the answer comes.

PRAYER FOR SURE THINGS AVOIDS PRESUMPTION

Presumption is to assume on God. When you pray for things that seem certain to happen anyway, you are showing God that you do not presume on His grace or mercy (cp. James 4:13-17). David earnestly prayed to be delivered from such pride, which he considered to be a 'great sin' (Psalm 19:13). Likewise, Jesus, in teaching His disciples to pray, encouraged them to pray even for those things which seemed assured to them (Luke 11:3). Too, consider Daniel the prophet. In Babylon, Daniel discovered through reading God's Word that the 70 years of captivity and punishment for the sins of his people were coming to an end. Nevertheless, Daniel prayed anyway for the forgiveness of the sins of his people (Daniel 9:2-19). He refused to presume upon God, but instead, stood upon God's *promise*, and prayed for that which God was already bringing to pass. Consider Isaac—he *knew* the promised son would come through his line, but still prayed about Rebekah's barrenness. He prayed for that which was already promised. Finally, there was Elijah, to whom God had promised rain. Not wanting to presume, Elijah prayed for rain anyway (I Kings 18:41-42).

PRAYER FOR SURE THINGS AVOIDS FATALISM

Sometimes we mistake the belief that God has the power to do whatever He chooses with mere fatalism. Fatalism is the attitude that says: "If God is going to do His perfect will in the universe, why should I even pray?" When you pray for sure things, you avoid this destructive philosophy. The fact that God has set His will in motion does *not* mean you and I don't have responsibilities *within* that plan (Acts 2:23; cp. Mark 14:21; cp. II Samuel 12:14-16). Fatalism sees everything as 'fixed', and prays for *nothing*. Praying for sure things shows God that you trust and depend on Him for *everything*, and take nothing for granted. Think of it this way. Because God says He has determined the precise length of your life (Psalm 90:12), should you therefore not eat or take care of yourself? Of course not. Similarly, even though God promised that His children would not have to endure His judgment on the world at history's end, He still instructs them to pray that they might escape (Luke 21:36). Remember, where fatalism sees your prayers as *unnecessary*, praying for sure things sees your prayers as being a wonderful *part* of God's perfect will (cp. Revelation 17:17).

PRAYER FOR SURE THINGS KEEPS US MORE OFTEN IN GOD'S COMPANY

If it did nothing else, praying for sure things keeps you in *constant* prayer. If you take *nothing* for granted, and pray for *everything*—as He instructs you to do—you will spend a great deal of time in communion with your Creator. God is never offended when you continue to ask Him to forgive your sins—even though He already has (Matthew 6:12; cp. Psalm 66:18; Proverbs 28:13). Asking for, and recognizing God's forgiveness for your sins, doesn't show a *lack* of faith in what He's done, but lets Him know you understand the *magnitude* of the achievement! On the other hand, don't feel that *not* asking forgiveness for your sins makes God stop forgiving you (I John 1:7). Remember, if God asks you to pray even for your daily bread, how *much* more, then, should you pray for the salvation which God has already assured you (II Peter 1:10)? Pray constantly. Staying in God's company is the finest company you could possibly keep!

PRAYER FOR SURE THINGS GIVES US AN OPPORTUNITY TO GLORIFY GOD

While praying for sure things is not an easy concept to understand, try to accept it as one of the most pleasing prayers you can offer God. It shows your *ultimate* dependence. Take care never to accept the 'sure thing' answers as automatic, or as things to be taken for granted. Instead, receive them in *submission* and *thanksgiving* as if the answers were miracles from God. This gives you another opportunity to glorify Him. Think of it this way: if you pray for *sure* things, and even for things which you may not be sure are even possible (cp. Mark 14:35-36), then if they *do* happen—you can offer special praise to God for answering your prayer. If they *don't* happen, at least you will know you did everything you could, and God said 'no'. You've wrapped every possibility in prayer, and in doing this, you glorify God.

PRAYER FOR SURE THINGS MIGHT ACTUALLY SPEED THE ANSWER

Finally, while we may never understand this concept, it might just be that when you pray for things certain to happen, they happen more *quickly* (cp. Revelation 22:20). We don't know God's timing on answering our prayers, but we can count on His promises coming to pass—maybe even *faster* if we pray!

My Blog!

We need to pray in all things—even when the answer seems sure. Don't presume on God. Make sure we're doing what He's told us to do. Prayer *might* speed the answer, and it *will* make us closer to God and bring glory to our Creator!

Heavenly Homework!

4me2cnsdr.now—

- Why is it important to pray for 'sure' things?

- What are you *leaning* on God for (*assuming* He will do) that you might better *request* of Him?

- Are there any things you are taking for granted (presuming on God for) each day?

- Why do you think God chooses to work *through* our prayers?

- When was the last time something good happened for which you were disappointed because you forgot to pray?

- When was the last time you thanked God for a sunny day, a gentle rain, a cool evening breeze, or just for giving you another day of life?

To do—

- ✓ Find something in your life that you are *sure* is in God's will and pray diligently for that to happen. When it does, be sure to praise God for it, and give Him the glory.

Instant Message Summary:

You need to pray even for the things that seem assured. These prayers evidence your complete and total faith and give you a unique and special opportunity to glorify God.

CHAPTER 11

"THE TRUE GRIT OF PRAYER"
ANSWERS DELAYED AND DENIED

FROM: JERRY
TO: GOD
SUBJECT: GOD, WHY DOES IT SOMETIMES SEEM YOU AREN'T LISTENING?

OK, God! Let me be frank. I've been praying lately, and I'm just not getting any answers! Are you there? It sure seems like you aren't listening. Have I gone wrong somehow? What should I be doing?

FROM: GOD
TO: JERRY
CC: THE CHURCH
SUBJECT: GOD, WHY DOES IT SOMETIMES SEEM YOU AREN'T LISTENING?

Jerry—Yes, I'm listening. Just because I am not giving you the answer immediately, or the answer you want, doesn't mean I'm not paying attention! You don't always get what you pray for, and sometimes, I am not even ready to say 'no'—I just want you to wait and keep praying. I AM here, I am listening, and I do love you! Just wait a bit.

Principle: God answers your every prayer. Sometimes He says 'yes'. Sometimes He says 'no'. But most of the time He says 'wait'. How you respond to God's answers reflects your trust in Him, and your ability to praise Him when the answer comes!

WHEN YOU THINK HE'S NOT LISTENING

God knows we are human, and get discouraged. He doesn't just turn us off when we get frustrated—even with Him—and question His ways. Neither does God chastise us when we sometimes doubt Him, or wonder if He even cares (Matthew 15:22-23; cp. Job 30:19-24). But remember, God *does* care, and He *will* answer your prayers (Matthew 7:7). And sometimes He answers even before you finish asking (Isaiah 65:24; cp. Daniel 10:12).

WHEN HIS ANSWER IF DIFFERENT FROM WHAT YOU EXPECTED

You may not always recognize God's answer to your prayers (Isaiah 55:8-9). Sometimes His answers are different from those you expect. Sometimes God answers—not by changing the situations you pray about—but by changing *you*, and your *perspective* of the situation (II Corinthians 12:8-9). Don't think God is not answering your prayer. It *is* an answer, and an answer wrapped in the grace to help you accept it. Remember too—when God finally does answer after making you wait—very often your blessing is *greater* than what you expected (I Samuel 1:11; 2:21). For example, Mary and Martha hoped Jesus would come in time to heal Lazarus from his sickness, but Jesus intentionally delayed so He could raise Lazarus from the dead (John 11:15; 44). In the same way, Jesus also intentionally delayed in coming to the daughter of Jairus. In both cases, people prayed for a *healing*, but received a *resurrection!*

GOD'S DELAY IS NOT GOD'S DENIAL

We live in a day of instant gratification. We want everything *now*. Most often when you pray, God does not immediately answer. You may see this as God not hearing you, or refusing your requests. But God's delay is not always God's denial. Often, your prayer was heard, but the *fulfillment* takes time (Daniel 10:12). Sometimes He's asking you to patiently wait so He can answer (Psalm 37:7; 40:1; cp. Luke 18:7) for your *good* (Lamentations 3:25). Sometimes God takes the time to work on the *other* end of your prayer (Daniel 10:13), and an immediate answer does not best suit His *will*, or your good. Even in Heaven some believers seem to be impatient waiting on God's timing (Revelation 6:10-11). God most often works (from our perspective) *in* time, *through* steps (I Kings 18:41-44). At such times, God is teaching you *patience, trust,* and *obedience.* Even Jesus had to learn obedience through His human nature (Hebrews 5:8). *Waiting* is a required course in your Christian school of life (James 1:4). Waiting doesn't *weaken* your faith— it *strengthens* it (Isaiah 40:31). Read in the Old Testament of how long Abraham,

Sarah, Isaac, Rebekah, Jacob, and Joseph were required to wait before God moved in *their* lives. Don't despair when God makes you wait. He hasn't forgotten you— He's *perfecting* you. Be patient. God *will* answer.

Accepting God's 'no'

It's hard to accept 'no' as an answer. It's *especially* hard to accept 'no' as an answer from God. Moses understood this (Deuteronomy 3:26) when He pleaded with God to enter the Promised Land. David understood this when God took his infant child in death because of the sin with Bathsheba (II Samuel 12:18). Paul understood this when God refused to heal him (II Corinthians 12:7-10). I understood this when I prayed for God to heal my mother of cancer, and she died. Sometimes, God simply says 'no' because He knows what's best for us (Romans 8:28), as in the case of denying Elijah's request to die. A denial for which the old prophet was most certainly grateful (I Kings 19:4-7)!

Accepting God's portion

Sometimes God answers, but not as *fully* as you might hope. In these instances, God may be giving you just enough so that you will have to trust Him for *more*. Joseph did this with his brothers in Egypt concerning the grain. As the famine became more intense, Joseph required them to return for more wheat when their limited supply was exhausted. Like God, Joseph did not limit the blessing to be *unkind*. He limited the blessing so that his brothers would have to *trust* him for more (Genesis 41:57; 43:1-2). In the same way, God gave limited manna to the Hebrews in the wilderness in order that they might trust Him for their *daily* bread (Exodus 16:19-21; cp, Matthew 6:11). While you may not understand *why* God limits your blessing, know that His plans for you are always for good (Jeremiah 29:11).

Understanding God's ultimate plan

God always answers your prayers. But He may have any number of reasons why He *delays*, says '*no*', or *measures* your blessing. Sometimes God never explains Himself (such as with Job). God's thoughts and plans are so much bigger than ours. God *is* the 'big picture', which we sometimes fail to remember (Isaiah 55:7-9). Nevertheless, God's ultimate plan *will* come to pass (Jeremiah 51:29), and is for your *good* and His *glory* (Jeremiah 29:11; cp. Romans 8:28). You may not see or understand His ultimate plan today (I Corinthians 13:12). Trust Him anyway. Some reasons behind God's dealings with us will never be known until Christ returns, but someday the mystery of His plan *will* be revealed (Revelation 10:7).

THANKING GOD THROUGH IT ALL

No matter how God answers your prayers, or how little you understand His ways, trust Him anyway, and pray because He *said* to. Do not steal glory from God (cp. Isaiah 42:8) by failing to thank Him—no matter how He answers. Trust God's character. He does everything right according to His perfect will (Ephesians 1:11; Psalm 37:5). Give *Him* full credit and praise (James 1:17; cp. Genesis 41:16). In this way, you will glorify Him—either for *answering* you—or for *trusting* you to wait, and you will never have a second thought about "…what might have happened if I had prayed?" Make an effort to thank God *before* He answers (cp. Daniel 6:10; Mark 11:24), and be sure you thank Him for hearing your prayers *at least* as often as you make requests in those prayers!

My Blog!

Accepting the timing and answers of God is not always an easy task. Sometimes we get that 'yes' answer, but more often, we are told 'no' or 'wait'. What we do with those answers is a barometer of our faith and reliance upon God. We need to be patient, and remember that He does not work according to our time schedule. But when God does answer, His plan is perfect.

Heavenly Homework!

4me2cnsdr.now—

- How has God ever changed your *perspective* on something through prayer?

- What is God asking you to wait for right now?

- When was the last time you thanked God for answering 'no' to a prayer?

- Do you spend more time *requesting* from God or *thanking* Him for what He's already done?

- How did you feel the last time God didn't answer your prayers the way you expected?

- Is there something God might be trying to teach you through waiting on Him?

- Have you ever felt guilty when you were surprised God actually answered a prayer? Why did you feel this way?

To do—

✓ The next time you pray for something and the answer is 'wait', try to praise God for that answer rather than question Him about it. See if there are lessons you can learn through waiting, and learn them the best you can. Give Him glory for this time of growth, and thank Him for it.

✓ Keep a journal of God's answered prayers. Look back on this in times of waiting.

Instant Message Summary:

Delay is not denial. Sometimes God isn't ready to share His plan with His children. Your job is to wait, trust Him and keep praying, giving God the glory.

CHAPTER 12

"THE SIGNATURE OF PRAYER"
THE AUTOGRAPH OF AUTHORITY

FROM: JERRY
TO: GOD
SUBJECT: HOW SHOULD I END MY PRAYERS?

I think I'm finally getting it, God, but one more question. I've heard a lot of people end their prayers with 'in Jesus' name. Amen.' Is that what I should say, and what exactly does this mean?

FROM: GOD
TO: JERRY
CC: THE CHURCH
SUBJECT: HOW SHOULD I END MY PRAYERS?

Jerry—When you finish praying, I want you to remember why you're even ABLE to come to Me with your requests! Remember, it's only because of the sacrifice of My Son for you! When you end your prayers, deliver them to Me through Him. Praying in His name or authority is not a special code, and it certainly doesn't have magical powers. But His name DOES remind you of the cost for the privilege of prayer, and that's what I want you to never forget.

Principle: Your prayers should always be offered as Christ would offer them—though obedience, trust, and concern for God's glory and perfect plan. Praying in the name of Jesus is to pray as Jesus would pray, and to recognize that He alone is the reason you can reach God's throne at all.

"For Christ's sake," and "in Jesus' name"

We close our discussion on prayer the same way we began it—stressing the glory of God and His Christ (Ephesians 3:21). For this reason, and to this end, you should tie up and send every prayer to God 'in the name of Jesus'. To pray in Jesus' name, or 'for Christ's sake' is not a mantra, formula, or good luck balloon attached to your prayer. Rather, it means to pray as Christ would pray—to know *His* mind—or to pray in the *Person, authority, relationship,* and *character* of the Son of God to His Father. God's name involves all God *is* (John 17:6). Remember, it is only because of Christ that you and I have access to God at all (Ephesians 2:18). He is our 'power of attorney' before God. Therefore, make *His* will *your* will (I Corinthians 2:16). To pray in Jesus' name means to pray as Jesus would pray, and Jesus always prayed with *God's* glory as the goal (John 17:4-8). When you are able to pray this way—in Christ's name—you can be assured that anything you ask will be answered (John 14:13-14; 15:16; 16:23-24; cp. I John 5:14-15).

In the ancient world, the name a mother gave her child comprised everything that was ever hoped or dreamed for that child in its lifetime. A person's name often reflected the *nature* of person it identified. For that reason, Moses understood that his people would want to know God's *name* (Exodus 3:13), or just *who* God was. For that reason too, we are warned not to use God (or Christ's) name *casually* (Deuteronomy 5:11). It is a *holy* and *awesome* name! Therefore, when you wrap your prayer in the name of Jesus, you present it to God in the *character* (holy, just, righteous, etc.), *Person* (the Son of God in the flesh), *power* (all-powerful and good), *promises* (to judge; to return, to bless), and *authority* of Christ (cp. II Corinthians 5:20). To *understand* the name of God is to *trust His character* (Psalm 9:10; cp. Psalm 20:7). Knowing this, be careful what you ask for.

Your ultimate goal and focus as you send your prayer to God is to glorify the Father and Christ—never forget that. Without Christ you can do *nothing* (John 15:5). With Him—*everything* is possible (Philippians 4:13). Trust in God, and develop old king Asa's attitude: "...we rest on thee, and in thy name" (II Chronicles 14:11). Give God full credit—even when it's hard—for hearing your prayer, *however* He chooses to answer. Entrust your prayer to His keeping and care with the assurance that He will be *faithful and true* (cp. Revelation 21:5; 22:6) in addressing your prayer—the very definition of the word 'Amen'. Wrap up your prayer and send it home 'in Christ'—Gods 'Amen'—and final expression of His love (Revelation 3:14).

My Blog!

As Christians, our new lives are in Jesus. So also should be our prayers! When we pray, we need to pray as *He* would pray. It's *His* will that counts! He alone has given us the privilege of approaching God. We need to always remember that!

Heavenly Homework!

4me2cnsdr.now—

- How do *you* wrap up your prayers and send them to God?

To do—

✓ The next time you end your prayer "in Jesus' name", ask yourself, "Is this *really* what Jesus would have prayed?" Did I try to find *His* will, and am I using this privilege well? What *would* Jesus do?

✓ Look up the many *names* for God in the Old Testament. Study His names and *attributes*. Learn about God's character.

Instant Message Summary:

Prayer is a privilege made possible for us through Christ. You are not holy enough in yourself to approach God. You need to keep in mind that when you pray, pray as *Christ* would pray, with *His* will as the prime objective.

CONCLUSION

Prayer is talking to God. Pray not only for your daily needs, but because God told you to. God wants you to be in constant fellowship with Him, not because He needs your company, but because you need His guidance. Prayer is a privilege reserved for the children of God, and should be grounded in faith, aligned with God's will, and delivered to the Father in the authority of His Son. Prayer should be simple, specific, directed from your heart to your loving Father, and void of formula and empty repetition. Effective prayer requires you to trust God totally, while doing everything you are able be a partial answer to your own requests. While it is not always easy, prayer's ultimate purpose is to glorify God for all He does, but more importantly, for Who He is.

About the Author

Jerry Parks has a Th.D from Trinity Theological Seminary, and is an ABF teacher at Southland Christian Church in Lexington, KY. Dr. Parks has also authored: *With Joseph in the University of Adversity: The Mizraim Principles*, based on principles from the life of Joseph the Hebrew in the Old Testament, and *Dragons, Grasshoppers & Frogs!*, a commentary for teenagers on the Book of Revelation.

Jerry may be contacted at kidztchr7@hotmail.com, or jhoo828@yahoo.com

978-0-595-40766-8
0-595-40766-8

Made in the USA
Lexington, KY
26 November 2016